Financial Co

Starting a Relationship
With the Right Advisor

Michael H Gross
CFP®, QPFC, CEBS, ChFC®, MSFS
President & Managing Principal
Cornerstone Corp.

Financial Planning
Investment Management
Retirement Plan Consulting

Printed in the United States of America

First Printing, 2016

ISBN 978-0-692-75125-1
Cornerstone Corp.

321 Townepark Circle

Louisville, KY 40243

www.CFP*wise*.com

CONTENTS

Introduction

Chances are, at some point during your formative years, your parents (or other trusted adults) sat you down to have "*the talk*". Not the one about the birds and the bees, rather the one they *hope* will set you up for relational success. It may have gone something like this:

> You know, young one, your mother and I want what's best for you, so we think it's time for us to share some good advice for finding your soul mate. We have put together a carefully crafted checklist – a few time-tested suggestions – to go by when selecting your life partner:

- ✓ Are the two of you compatible?
- ✓ Is he/she a respectable member of society?
- ✓ Do you share the same values and goals?
- ✓ Is he/she trustworthy?
- ✓ Will he/she set you up for success in life?

I'm sure it sounded reasonable at the time, as is most wisdom handed down from our elders, but what about the non-love relationships in your life? What about a courtship checklist for finding, say, a doctor, pastor, or legal professional? What about the ever-important financial relationships you'll seek? Indeed, what about *Financial Courtship*?

Granted, your relationship with a financial advisor doesn't exactly rise to the level of *marriage,* as our "courtship" metaphor implies. But, like strong marriages, advisor-client partnerships are long-term commitments, centered on compatibility, mutual respect, shared values, and trust.

Maybe you've already tried your hand at *Financial Courtship* (i.e. finding a qualified Planner or Advisor to help you along the way), but were left discouraged, disappointed, and confused. Like a marriage gone wrong, a relationship with the *wrong* advisor can end badly, and leave behind a trail of unwelcome consequences. As such, many otherwise prudent people are forgoing financial partnerships altogether for a "Do-It-Yourself" approach. Unfortunately, when it comes to financial planning, *Do-It-Yourselfers* can find themselves with underperforming investments and underfunded retirement savings. When it comes to *your* personal wealth and financial security – a learn-as-you-go approach is quiet simply a bad idea.

In lieu of the fact that you are reading this book *right now,* I am going to assume that you are aware of those pit-falls and are ready to find *your* perfect financial partner. You have made a wise decision. Nevertheless, I do need to caution you. Even though you may have the best of intentions *right now*, the first obstacle that most people encounter, as they begin thinking about planning for retirement, is overcoming their own procrastination. The thought of navigating temperamental economies, changing interest rates, volatile stock markets, inflation fears, global geo-political risks, and widespread conflicting financial advice can be intimidating – especially under a constantly shrinking time horizon. When it comes to saving for retirement, the proverbial clock keeps ticking – a metaphor not lost on our "marriage" analogy.

Ignoring the problem – even for a few years – is not a reasonable solution. Sure, the *easiest* thing to do *right now* may be to do nothing. After all, you may not be retiring tomorrow. But we know that procrastinating is not the *right* thing to do. As each year passes, retirement age draws nearer, and the magic of compound interest starts to lose its power. The less *time* you have between *now* and the time you begin relying on your retirement income, the more limited your planning options become.

The time to get up, get going, get help, and get *winning* is now! *Right now.*

Even if you've procrastinated in planning up to this point (as many of us have), or feel way behind in total savings (as many of us do), there's still time. You can get from where you are to where you want to be. By finding the right financial professional *now*, you are more likely to get on track towards your own financial independence. The retirement lifestyle you have hoped for *can* become a reality.

Besides, what other options do you realistically have for retiring with enough resources to fund your future?

- Win the lottery?
- Rely on family and friends?
- Expect the government to take care of you?

The truth is, no one *accidentally* achieves financial independence. It is an *intentional* and *purposeful* exercise in prudence, planning, and perseverance; an exercise best executed with someone who *knows* what they are doing.

You need a *Financial Partner*!

Sure, you could forgo finding a qualified advisor and instead spend countless hours pouring over financial textbooks, attending boring seminars, or cruising the web in an effort to grasp Estate Planning, Income

Taxes, Investment Strategies, Social Security Benefits, Medicare Madness, Insurance Planning, and more. But, let's be honest, you're not likely to get around to it because: (a) there are more fun things to do in life (except for geeks like me), and (b) if you were going to do it, you would have done it by now.

The bottom line is this: Your choice to hire the right advisor is perhaps the single most important decision of your financial life. *And*, the longer you wait to find *Mr. or Mrs. Right,* the more costly and less probable funding your retirement becomes.

The difference between getting involved with just *any-ole* advisor and *the right* advisor can mean the difference between retiring on time and being financially independent, or struggling just to make ends meet. That is why the Courtship Criteria outlined in Part I of this easy to read handbook - *Financial Courtship* - is so important. These guidelines will empower you to choose a financial partner that will help you navigate the ups-and-downs of our economy, plan for the various seasons of your life, and fund your future dreams.

In addition to the Courtship Criteria in Part I, Part II consists of "Nine Questions to Ask an Advisor" *before* you make a commitment. You'll find a helpful "Courtship Checklist" at the end of each section.

My goal is to equip you with the tools you need to make the right decision when choosing *your* financial partner!

Author Note: On distinguishing professional titles. There are nuanced differences in those who hold themselves out as "Financial Planner", "Wealth Manager", "Investment Advisor", etc. However, for the purpose of this short book, I'll hereby refer to anyone seeking to help you with your finances as a *Financial Advisor.*

PART I

Your Financial Courtship Criteria

Criteria 1

Screen Your Candidates

When pre-screening your potential life partner, chances are your Mom and Dad had some strong "feelings" on the subject. Their basic criteria might have looked something like this:

- ✓ Selfless and Caring
- ✓ Treats you with Love and Respect
- ✓ Shares your Values and Goals
- ✓ Wants what you want out of life
- ✓ Upstanding Citizen

However, what are some pre-screening criteria you can consider before going on a first date with a potential *financial* life partner? The answer is *the same checklist as above!* But you can add to that list:

- ✓ Education Background
- ✓ Professional Credentials
- ✓ Experience

Education

Did you know that a college degree in Personal Finances is *not* a legal requirement to give financial advice? The sad truth is that a high percentage of so-called "experts" in this field, do not even have a related college degree.

The minimum requirement you should expect from your advisor, in terms of education, is either a Bachelor's degree in Business Science (BBS) or Business Administration (BBA). However, if you want the best of the best, look for an advisor with a Graduate (Master's) Degree in Personal Financial Planning. You may have to look a little harder, but a Master's Degree suggests an in-depth knowledge of the subject matter as well as a profound seriousness about financial planning as a profession.

Unfortunately, many people end up working as financial professionals by way of a 2nd or even 3rd career choice, while others are attracted by large financial institutions who need people to sell their proprietary products. These companies generally have very low barriers to entry, hiring most anyone willing to sell for commissions. The important thing to remember, regarding a candidate's formal education, is to screen for knowledge, commitment, and financial-specific academic training.

Credentials

Our instinct is to create mental shortcuts to vet a professional's level of expertise. One way we do this is by looking for an important-sounding job title, or familiar-sounding initials (credentialed "letters") after the person's name. While this may be a reasonable starting point, it should not be the *sole* basis for your selection.

Many professional titles (i.e. how someone holds themselves out to the public) are more self-assigned marketing labels, than representations of actual authority, responsibility, or job function. So while working directly with the "Vice President of Investments" may sound enticing, it doesn't guarantee that person is competent at managing your life's savings.

And what then are we to make of all those little initials (letters) after an advisor's name?

The ugly truth is that many *for-profit marketing programs* have invented, and allow advisors to use, their lettered credentials simply for paying a few hundred bucks, attending a weekend seminar, and passing an easy *self-proctored* exam. Unfortunately, these "weekend-credentials" exist alongside bona-fide designations that, by contrast, are quite rigorous to achieve, require substantial continued education, and may take *years* (not weekends) to complete. These latter, more widely accepted credentials, generally require passing ethical background checks and involve heavily-proctored examinations ... sometimes lasting *days*.

Below are a few industry standard-bearers that are widely accepted as proving high levels of competence (in the areas of money management or personal finances):

- CFP – Certified Financial Planner
- CFA – Chartered Financial Analyst
- ChFC – Chartered Financial Consultant

An advisor with one or more of these credentials deserves your consideration.

Experience
Look for an advisor who is highly committed to a life-long career path of serving the financial needs of others. Experience that spans more than a decade will insure that your advisor has navigated more than one significant market downturn ("*bear*" market) during their career. Knowing how to handle volatile shifts in the market without losing one's cool is not taught, but rather is learned through experience.

The most obvious demonstration of this is to find out how long your candidate has been in the profession. Sadly, ours is an industry that experiences high turnover, due in large part to the difficulty of becoming effective and competent in the field.

Be sure to *ask* how many years the advisor has been offering financial guidance directly to individuals and families. It's a fair and relevant question. This is *not* like working with a doctor who recently completed their residency. Even newly minted Physicians have undergone extremely rigorous academic and hands-on testing in their fields of specialty. They don't get to wear the white coats with "Dr." stitched on the front after passing a few weekend exams. Even a new doctor has the equivalent of a *decade* of experience.

Also, don't let the "big-name" of a financial firm fool you. Many of the largest brand name financial and investment companies constantly hire new – and inexperienced – advisors to fill their ranks. Indiscriminate hiring feeds their growth and profit motives, but not necessarily *your* retirement goals. This pertains to big Wall-Street brokerage houses, many banks, and especially insurance companies. Just because you've heard of the parent company, doesn't mean the advisor you would be working with has the necessary experience, talent, or skills.

Think logically, objectively, and unemotionally about whom to trust with your financial future. Pre-screening your candidates by looking into their education, credentials, and experience *before* you go on that first date, will help insure you are courting the *right* Financial Advisor.

> KEY TAKEAWAY: Don't hire a candidate *before* you have thoroughly vetted them. Do hire a candidate with the right education, experience, and credentials.

Criteria #1 – Screening Candidates

✔ CHECK LIST

☐ Education (one or more of the following):

BS – Bachelors of Science in Business

MBA/MSFS – Graduate/Master's Degree

☐ Credentials (rigorous "gold standards"):

CFP - Certified Financial Planner

CFA – Chartered Financial Analyst

ChFC – Chartered Financial Consultant

☐ Experience:

10+ years Financial Planning & Advice

Proven Results (ask for referrals

Criteria 2

Seek Compatibility

Interviewing an advisor candidate in person is like going on a first date. The advisor may have looked great on paper (just as a romantic connection might have looked great on-line). Nothing, however, compares to that first, all-important, face-to-face meeting.

A few questions you should keep in mind when sitting across the table from the candidate are:

- ✓ Do I really like this person?
- ✓ Can I spend time with this person?
- ✓ Do I get a sense of trustworthiness?
- ✓ Do I feel comfortable around him/her?
- ✓ Are they attentive and a good listener?
- ✓ Are we compatible?

Psychologists and psychiatrists can probably tell us *why* we feel more "*comfortable*" with one type of person verses another, but often it comes down to basic instinct. What is your gut telling you?

There's no shame in foregoing a key hiring decision due to a "*funny feeling*" you get from the candidate. Chances are your instincts are correct. After all, for a healthy long-term advisor-client relationship to work properly, your personalities need to be compatible. You will be spending time together. You will be sharing intensely personal information with this person. You will be looking to this advisor to help build your financial future...through good times and bad.

Getting into a relationship with an advisor who makes you feel uncomfortable, or who doesn't share your values, is never a good idea – no matter what he's promising or how qualified he might otherwise appear.

To determine a *good* compatibility fit, first ask yourself a few questions:

- Which personality style suits me best - someone with a teacher's heart, or a gifted and dynamic speaker?
- Am I looking for a sympathetic ear, or a straightforward coach?
- Do I want someone to walk alongside me and my goals, or a leader to show me the way and light the path?

Being self-reflective, and knowing the personality type that you are most compatible with will greatly benefit your courtship process.

KEY TAKEAWAY: Don't hire a candidate who is unprofessional, makes you feel uncomfortable, or intimidated. Do hire an advisor who is trustworthy, professional, and makes you feel comfortable and at ease.

Criteria #2 – Seek Compatibility

✔ CHECK LIST

- ☐ He / She is Likable
- ☐ He / She is Trustworthy
- ☐ He / She is Professional
- ☐ We are Compatible

Criteria 3

Too Good To Be True

You have probably heard the old adage, *if it's too good to be true, then it probably is.*

This is good advice when it comes to selecting a potential financial partner.

Too many eager believers have jumped into bed with flashy advisors making big promises and boasting unheard of returns, only to discover they've been had. Ever heard of Bernie Madoff? Enough said!

While guys like Bernie have made it difficult for the rest of us, the truth is the vast majority of advisors are *not* running complicated "Ponzi" schemes. The vast majority of advisors are well-intentioned professionals who sincerely care about their clients. The question is, how can *you* tell the difference?

A good rule of thumb: Anyone dangling the promise of ridiculously high returns, poised to outpace the markets, *proceed with caution.*

Very few - I mean very few - advisors are able to outperform the markets over time. Don't let the promise of high returns be the sole criteria by which you make this all important partnership decision.

Sober minded and honest professionals will offer you a clear and realistic picture of what you can expect from your mutual relationship. Anyone promising you the world, without a realistic plan, is perhaps *not the one* you want to court, let alone "marry".

> KEY TAKEAWAY: Don't hire a candidate who boasts outrageous returns without serious due diligence. Do hire an advisor who offers comprehensive planning, realistic returns, and personalized attention, and always ask for references.

Criteria #3 – Too Good To Be True

✔ CHECK LIST

☐ It did not sound "*too good to be true*"

☐ I was given several reputable references

Criteria 4

Never Rush In

Advisors should carry strong convictions with respect to recommendations, without waffling or wavering. However, any advice that requires *urgency*, or urgent *action*, should be looked at suspiciously, regardless of the rationale. Rushed decisions are made when emotions are misguided or when prudent analysis has been circumvented. You are wise to avoid advisors who pressure you to *hurry up and sign now*.

Slow down, take a deep breath, and relax before making major decisions that have the power to shape your financial future. For every consequential move in life (financial, relational, or otherwise) it is wise to practice prudent deliberation, careful due diligence, and even just "sleeping on it".

Whenever you hear a financial person urging you to "*act quickly*" in order to take advantage of some urgent opportunity, take a step back and *press the pause button*. You should never be coerced with the threat of a looming deadline, nor should you act out of fear of missing out on something "*big*". That is not how long-term investing works.

While they won't come out and say it, advisors who pressure you to act quickly are probably soliciting one of two ideas in you: Either you'll miss out on something everyone else is successfully taking advantage of; or by not acting soon, you're subject to probable financial harm. These are fear tactics that evoke emotions rather than logic, and are often toxic.

The financial markets are mainly efficient, meaning any real *opportunities* (stock price anomalies, for example) quickly adjust to new information available to the general public. "*Hot Stocks*" that are *poised to move,* along with short-term market predictions, are sales tactics that play into two powerful human motivators: fear and greed.

Fear says, "*I'll miss out and stay poor,*" while Greed says, "*I'll get rich if I put all my eggs in this one perfect basket.*"

The truth is, nobody really knows what the market is going to do from day to day, or even year-to-year. While it's important to gauge whether broad economic conditions are favorable or unfavorable at a given point in time, the prudent investor is better off focusing on long-term risk and reward, rather than short-term chances and odds.

Perhaps more importantly, waiting around for *insider information* on a so-called "hot stock" poised to explode into the stratosphere, is not only imprudent, but potentially *illegal.*

The bottom line is this, *never* rush your financial courtship, but also don't be a chronic "dater" either. Putting off this important relationship decision indefinitely is never a good idea.

> KEY TAKEAWAY: Don't hire an advisor who "rushes" you into a decision. Do hire and advisor who is thorough and patient with you. Someone you can trust.

Criteria #4 – Never Rush In

✔ CHECK LIST

☐ I Do Not Feel Rushed

☐ He / She Has Been Thorough and Patient

Criteria 5

Clarity & Understanding

There's beauty in simplicity.

Here's a good rule of thumb: *Do you understand everything the advisor is saying, and grasp what it means for you?*

The overall financial plan, products, goals, and timelines being proposed should be crystal clear. This holds true even – and especially - if you're not well versed in financial matters, or have little experience dealing with money management. Look for guidance that is free and clear of industry jargon, and absent undue complexity.

Most financial planning topics, such as taxation, investments, economics, estate planning, and risk management, are inherently complex. Therefore, a great test of an advisor's true *expertise* is his or her ability to understand the subject so well as to *reduce* that complexity into a simple explanation.

Albert Einstein's famous "$E=MC^2$" equation provided the layperson an easy, yet elegant, way to understand how mass and energy relate to each other (i.e. *relativity*). But the underlying theories supporting how he got there are anything but simple. In this way, finding a financial advisor whom you fully understand puts you in a more confident position to *win with money,* without all the mind-numbing details behind it.

There are a few possible reasons why advice is often *not* presented in a clear and concise manner (and none of them are good):

(1) Advisors themselves don't really understand how their recommendations work;
(2) They don't want *you* to fully comprehend it, because they're hiding something;
(3) They do understand it, but just lack good teaching or communication skills.

You will recognize this last one when the advisor tries to *appear* smart, showing off his knowledge by using big words to impress you, and making assumptions about your comprehension. Unfortunately, this approach may leave *you* feeling confused and overwhelmed.

Never put your hard earned money into something until you *understand how it works.* That doesn't mean you need all the trivial details before acting in good faith. It means you should at least have a good handle on the key concepts, main purpose, costs, tradeoffs, and overall benefits of recommendations, *before* moving forward with the decision.

Very few people are taught financial and investment planning concepts growing up. So there's no reason you should expect yourself *naturally* to know how to build and protect wealth. The value of a good financial advisor is to walk alongside you, coach you, teach you, and counsel you until you are comfortable enough to make the right financial decisions.

> KEY TAKEAWAY: Don't hire an advisor who is unclear, or whom you don't fully understand. Do hire someone who presents advice clearly.

Criteria #5 – Clarity & Understanding

✔ CHECK LIST

- ☐ He / She Has Clearly Explained the Plan
- ☐ I Understand the Proposed Plan

Criteria 6

Beware of Premature Advice

Suppose you meet with a financial advisor *for the very first time,* and early in the conversation you are presented with solutions and recommendations. Advice that is given prematurely, in advance of thorough discovery and deliberation, has a great chance of being *wrong.* Without adequate knowledge of your resources, goals, risk tolerances, and liquidity needs, premature financial advice is to be taken with a grain of salt, or perhaps not taken at all.

Off-the-cuff advice may *appear* on the surface to be suitable, especially when it comes from a professional. But unless an advisor takes the time to gather all relevant data and interview you about your needs and wants, solutions are likely to be self-serving (*the advisor's* self, not yours!).

In my opinion, it's wise practice for advisors to avoid offering *any* definitive financial solutions until there's been enough time to run the math and consider all the alternatives. We call that *shooting holes* in the advice, whereby a planning team deliberates and "stress-tests" various recommendations (outside the presence of the client). Advisors need to see potential pitfalls from all angles. This takes time.

There are untold gems an advisor will unearth during a patient, in-depth discussion with you. Exploring your financial background, family dynamics, risk profile, available resources, tax situation, and estate organization, not only brings insight, but also *perspective* for your planner.

Here are a few examples of advice given prematurely, without perspective, and in danger of robbing you of the best solutions:

- An advisor recommends you buy life insurance, but neglects to inquire about your employee group benefits at work.
- An advisor recommends that you draft a Simple Will for your Estate Plan, but wasn't aware that you have a special-needs child, or that you own assets in another state.
- An advisor suggests that you invest in a tax-deferred annuity, but didn't realize that you plan to retire early, and may need more flexible access to that money.

You get the idea.

KEY TAKEAWAY: Don't hire an advisor who is too impatient to inventory your whole situation and needs. Do hire an advisor who takes his/her time, does his/her due diligence, gets to know you, and tracks with your goals and values.

Criteria #6 – Beware of Premature Advice

✔ CHECK LIST

- ☐ I Was Not Offered Advice Prematurely
- ☐ He / She Has Done Due Diligence

Criteria 7

Avoid Tunnel Vision

Tunnel Vision is closely related to Premature Advice, but with one key distinction:

> Premature Advice is when recommendations are given *before* all the necessary facts and data are on the table. *Tunnel Vision*, on the other hand, is when advice is limited in scope to a single planning subject or tool.

When you hire a professional for financial advice, it is important to know the *extent* and *scope* of that advice. *Scope* refers to how many different subjects are being covered (e.g. tax planning, estate planning, insurance planning, investment planning, cash and debt management, retirement planning, employee benefits, etc.). *Extent* refers to the depth of advice within each of those subjects. You can think of it this way:

Extent = Deep
Scope = Wide

If you're looking for a true financial partner, one who will walk alongside you through the many – and ever changing – life seasons, hire someone with *comprehensive* training, broad expertise, and a diverse educational background. In other words, seek advice that is *both deep and wide.*

This is important because individual facets of your personal finances are *interconnected* with other aspects of your financial plan. Changes to one area often has unintended – and often delayed – negative consequences.

Here are some examples:

- Changes to your Investment Strategy impacts your taxes.
- Changes to your Life Insurance affects your Estate Plan.
- Changes to your Employee Benefits may change your Retirement security.

Tunnel Vision (i.e. single-module advice), therefore, can be problematic. Just know that whatever changes you make to your overall financial plan can adversely affect your portfolio and/or create unintended consequences down the road.

Be cautious! There is an epidemic of sales people out there holding themselves out as "Financial Planners". Some are worthy; more than a few are not. If an insurance product, for example, seems to be the primary focus, beware. Similarly, if gathering investment assets seems to encapsulate the entirety of the "planning" advice, seek guidance elsewhere.

Having spent many years practicing *comprehensive* Financial Planning, I highly recommend you work with a Certified Financial Planner (CFP®). Regardless of the scope and extent of your current needs, chances are, a CFP® will be looking at your needs from many different angles. Moreover, CFP®'s are duty-bound (under oath) to review and consider your overall financial circumstances, even before making very minor suggestions.

> KEY TAKEAWAY – Don't hire an advisor who isn't qualified to address your comprehensive planning needs. Do seek financial guidance from a Certified Financial Planning professional.

Criteria #7 – Avoid Tunnel Vision

✔ CHECK LIST

☐ He / She is qualified to offer comprehensive planning advice

Criteria 8

Customized, Not Canned

Beware of the advisor who attempts to solve all the world's financial problems with a single product – a "one-size-fits-all" – fix. This *one-trick-pony* advisor may be more concerned with hitting his production and income goals, than with finding thoughtful solutions aimed at *your* objectives.

Discernment and deliberation are the two cornerstones of building customized financial recommendations. It's not that one idea can't work for you; it's when that one idea is sold to *everyone* the advisor meets with...*every time.*

While financial *education* can be given generally, personalized financial *advice* cannot. Your story is different than everyone else's, and thus your pathway to success will be different also. For this reason, it is wise to seek counsel from an unbiased, and independent, financial advisor.

Partner with an advisor who has unencumbered freedom to shop around for the very best solutions to match your objectives. Never underestimate the power of incentives when it comes to a financial firm's (and their employees') bias towards pushing products that align with *their* interest, not yours.

A good advisor will begin by addressing your financial goals and objectives, and then work to find solutions using *multiple* products and strategies that fit various life stages. You may end up selecting only one idea at a time, but it's always wise to consider different options, before implementing the ones that make most sense *right now.*

The advisor's role, therefore, is to patiently explain each of the best possible options, teaching you the similarities and differences along the way, before making a *definitive* recommendation.

Conversely, it is *not* appropriate for an advisor to provide a virtual showroom of possible options and say, "*Now you decide.*" Good counsel includes guiding you to the *very best* possible course of action – indeed, the action he himself would take, were he in your exact financial position. After all, that is what you are paying the advisor to do.

KEY TAKEAWAY: Don't hire an advisor who has a canned solution to all financial issues, or who works for a company pushing proprietary products. Do hire an advisor who is free to offer the best combination of solutions to custom-fit your needs.

Criteria #8 – Customized, Not Canned

✔ CHECK LIST

- ☐ Solutions are not One Size Fits All.
- ☐ He / She is Free to Offer Me a Customized and Comprehensive Plan

Criteria 9

Expect Full Disclosure

Just like relational and romantic courtships, *full disclosure* from your financial planner is critical *before* you make a commitment to invest or buy products from him/her. Sadly, advisors neglecting to give a client all the facts before they invest (*acts of omission)* are common sales tactic used by less scrupulous professionals. Unfortunately, it can take years before any "*acts of omission*" are discovered, by then it may be too late to reverse the effects of what was *left out* of those early discussions.

For example, wouldn't you find it relevant to know about any penalties or restrictions to accessing (withdrawing) your money, *before* opening an account? Or wouldn't you like to know if an insurance carrier had the ability to raise premiums at any time, *before* taking out the policy?

Fortunately, acts of omission are sometimes unintentional, and not the product of deception. The advisor may not have even known about all those missing details when they offered their recommendations. This suggests *negligence* more than *malice*. But that doesn't change the impact to your portfolio or to your financial security.

It is the role of the *advisor* to sift through the minutia and highlight anything that is meaningful and material to your making a financial decision. Advisors are duty-bound to do this, even though many avoid this step. While some advisors *intentionally hide* material facts (e.g. fees, risks, taxes, etc.), most neglect full disclosure out of simple carelessness and/or inexperience.

The truth is, there is not a single financial planning or investment management strategy that doesn't have some sort of tradeoff or limitation. It may have to do with higher costs, illiquidity, inflexibility, added complexity, or lower expected returns, but it is always there...*somewhere.* Therefore, the *absence* of pointing out such tradeoffs is the telltale sign something is amiss.

Here are two examples:

(1) Your advisor recommends a Roth IRA for the tax free growth...but neglects to mention that you can't touch the earnings for five years or age 59 ½, without penalties.
(2) Your advisor proposes a Variable Annuity for the guaranteed growth of retirement

income...but does not disclose the higher expenses and liquidity restrictions.

The preceding examples do not suggest that the advice was necessarily *wrong*, just *incomplete*. Complete advice always exposes the material tradeoffs, risks, and limitations. And, again, they are always there! So the only way to know if something is being *left out* of a financial proposal is to observe whether the solution seems *too-good-to-be-true*. If all you are hearing are the positive aspects of an investment proposal or financial strategy, without any reference to potential tradeoffs or risks, you are wise to question thc one presenting it.

> KEY TAKEAWAY – Don't hire an advisor who gives you only *good news*. That advisor is bad news. Do hire an advisor who is honest and shares the whole balanced picture, not just the benefits.

Criteria #9 – Expect Full Disclosure

✔ CHECK LIST

☐ My advisor has talked to me about all the tradeoffs and limitations of my plan.

Criteria 10

Count The Cost

Costs associated with financial management, investment advice, and other account services can be difficult to calculate, and even harder to *find.* Some fees are within the advisors control, while others are not. Either way, it's incumbent upon the *advisor* – not you – to outline any and all management expenses, fees, or anything else that has the effect of reducing your net portfolio returns.

The world is littered with unscrupulous brokers and advisors who systematically downplay, and often *hide* material information about the total cost of investing and money management. Good advisors will be more open and forthright about discussing fees and expenses – and not just the ones *they* charge, but any others your accounts are subject to.

The truth is, it's neither *ethical* nor *legal* to knowingly conceal material information relevant to a client making an investment decision. This truth provides you with a *minimum* baseline for assessing fees.

When courting a financial advisor, the conversation about fees should be straightforward:

- What does the advisor charge?
- What does the advisor's firm charge?
- What additional 3rd party, custodial, trading, or assessments are charged?

Additionally, ask about any upfront loads or back-end commissions. All of these costs reduce the net amount of money going to work in your investment portfolio. Once you add up all the costs, the total is an annual percentage of assets under management.

The next step is to simply take the *projected* annual portfolio return, and *reduce it* by your total costs (fees & expenses). This is your *net expected return.*

Example:

> You have $100,000 to invest. Your total fees and expenses add up to 2.75% per year. If your expected return is 10%, your *actual* return will be only 7.25%. This may sound fair, until you consider the effect of compounding over, say, 10, 20, or even 30-years. *Return-reducing fees* certainly add up over time...and can mean the difference between retiring well, and retiring *very* well.

I suggest that you look for an advisor who openly welcomes the conversation about costs, fees, and expenses. Honestly, the topic of fees and compensation should come up early in the *first meeting.* If it doesn't, be prepared to ask this question:

> *"If I were to invest my hard-earned money, with your firm managing my accounts, what fees can I expect, and what services do those fees include?"*

Their answer to this should tell you –

(1) Whether the advisor even knows what all the fees are, and can explain their purpose.
(2) Whether the advisor is primarily fee-based or commission-based. In other words, is his first loyalty to *you* as a fiduciary (fee-based), or to his *company* as a sales rep (commission-based)
(3) Whether the fees are *reasonable* based on the level of *experience* they have, and the total *services* they intend to provide.

> KEY TAKEAWAY – Count the cost when hiring a financial partner. Don't hire an advisor who dodges the conversation about fees. Do hire an advisor who is *up-front and honest* with you about all costs and expenses associated with your plan.

Criteria #10 – Count The Cost

✓ CHECK LIST

☐ The Advisor Talked to Me About Fees

☐ The Advisor Charges ________

☐ The Advisors Firm Charges _______

☐ Are There 3rd Party Charges? Yes No

- If Yes, what are they? _________________________

☐ Are There Upfront Loads or Commissions? *Yes No*

- If Yes, what are they? _________________________

☐ My Annual Net Return, Less Charges is: ______

Your Working Check List

- ☐ I Screened My Candidate
- ☐ We Are Compatible
- ☐ It Was Not *Too Good To Be True*
- ☐ I Did Not Feel Rushed
- ☐ There Is Clarity & Understanding
- ☐ I Did Not Take Premature Advice
- ☐ I Avoided Tunnel Vision Advice
- ☐ The Proposal is Customized, Not Canned
- ☐ I Received Full Disclosure
- ☐ I Know All The Costs
- ☐ I'm Ready for a Committed Relationship

PART II

Nine Questions
To Ask When Courting
a Financial Advisor

Nine Questions To Ask When Courting a Financial Advisor

Before hiring a *financial advisor* (the person to whom you're about to trust with your financial future and life savings), it is wise to be prepared with a few good interview questions, in advance of your first meeting.

Asking the following *Nine Questions* will help you separate the *good* advisors from the *bad*, and will steer the conversation away from product sales, and towards a more meaningful dialogue. How an advisor answers these *Nine Questions,* will give you a better sense of your compatibility – both personal and financial.

Answers you receive in response to these *Nine Questions* can range from confusing to enlightening, so I've added some guidance on what to listen for (*Preferred Answers*), as well as general context (*Why this is Important*).

Question #1

Who will be my primary point of contact for financial advice?

Preferred Answer:

"Me!" (The person you are interviewing)

Look for an answer that suggests you'll be working directly (one-on-one) with the most experienced senior Advisor, sometimes called the firm's *Principal.* Usually, that's the person you're interviewing, but not always.

Why this is Important:

Don't fall for a *bait & switch*, whereby a senior advisor meets with you in the beginning, but then hands your account off to a less experienced *Junior* or *Associate* advisor. Accountability means that the person sharing the vision with you is the same person on the hook for the results.

Question #2

How do you measure performance?

Preferred Answer:

"We measure performance in terms of *actual outcomes* (i.e. planning results). *Good* performance, to us, means that your goals and objectives are being met with the least amount of risk and cost."

Why this is Important:

When advisors – and some clients – think of *performance*, they often think only in terms of investment returns. However, holistic performance results should be measured against whether or not progress is being made towards the *needs, wants,* and long-term *objectives* of your financial plan. Those types of metrics are hard to fake. You either succeed at accomplishing your financial goals, or not. You either meet your objectives with minimal risk, or you don't.

Question #3

How do you handle service requests?

Preferred Answer:

"Quickly and accurately."

Why this is Important:

You're not just hiring the advisor, but the whole support staff too. Providing accurate and thoughtful financial advice is demanding enough. Trying to do that while also processing paperwork, scheduling meetings, changing beneficiaries, and moving money into your checking account is more than any one person can – or *should* – do alone. It's simply not efficient for an advisor to handle basic service tasks that are unrelated to financial or investment strategies. A "team effort" is vital in that regard. The things to listen for are responsiveness, attention to detail, and a systematic set of internal processes for handling service-related issues.

Talk is cheap. Ten out of ten financial advisors will probably tell you how great their service is, and how fast they respond to clients' needs. I would... and do. But there's simply no way to *prove* (or disprove) that in advance. So it's important to discuss *specific* processes, formal policies, and dedicated resources, rather than speak vaguely about best intentions.

For instance, how long before sending an email or voicemail can you expect a call back? For administrative needs, who will be your primary point of contact, someone local or an 800-number? Note that all investment and financial planning related questions should be handled directly by your personal *advisor*. This includes phone calls, review meetings, and financial updates. Good advisors may have many clients, but you should always feel like *your* needs come first (because they do!).

Question #4

Where will my money
be held for safekeeping?

Preferred Answer:

"Your accounts will be held at _____" [*insert name of recognized custody & clearing firm*]

...But then the advisor should clarify what you mean by "*safekeeping*".

Why this is Important:

Asset custodians have the job of holding onto your securities (investments). They process transactions, collect dividends, pay interest to the account, and report performance (often monthly or quarterly). Many custodians are familiar names like Fidelity, Charles Schwab, and Pershing, or *Wirehouses* like Merrill Lynch or UBS.

Most brokerage accounts are protected by SIPC (Securities Investor Protection Corp.). SIPC acts somewhat like FDIC (Federal Deposit Insurance Corp.) at banks, but with one key difference: While Federal Deposit Insurance (FDIC) actually protects the value of deposits, SIPC only protects against the loss of securities and deposits due to custodial insolvency, not against the securities decline in market value. The *real* safety of your account is determined by the *selection* of investments (usually as recommended by the advisor).

Question #5

What's your perspective on *risk*, and what efforts will you take to understand mine?

Preferred Answer:

"Risk can't be eliminated, but it should be *managed* (along with your expectations). We'll work hard to accurately measure your tolerance of *and* capacity for short-term investment losses. We will build a suitable investment plan which maximizes potential *gains* within those risk boundaries."

Why this is Important:

Basically, the advisor needs to articulate a *balanced perspective* of risk, and recognize that many different categories of risk affect investment planning (beyond the obvious stock market risks). Additionally, advisors should not substitute their personal risk profiles for that of yours. An advisor's situation – and professional knowledge – is likely very different from your own.

You're probably familiar with the concept *risk-of-loss*. This is simply the risk that an investment can decline in value, whether on paper or when you go to withdraw it. *Risk-of-loss* can also refer to investments that underperform against expectation, or even investments that were never made in the first place (*opportunity cost*).

While your comfort level (tolerance) for risk can be measured by profile questionnaires, your *capacity* for risk, on the other hand, is uncovered through a thorough Financial Planning process. A good advisor will understand *both* of these risk assessments well enough to effectively manage investments on your behalf.

Question #6

Are there any costs or surrender penalties for leaving your firm or closing my account?

Preferred Answer:

"No, none at all."

"If you aren't satisfied for any reason, there won't be any costs, penalties, or hard feelings if we simply part ways".

Why this is Important:

Certain types of investment accounts and financial products pay the advisor an up-front commission (or "load") in exchange for locking your money up for a specified period of time. These *liquidity restrictions* often come with a fee or penalty for withdrawing your money too soon, before the surrender period ends. It's not that these accounts or products are necessarily *bad*, but given the choice of *flexibility or not*, it's best to keep your options open.

One way to hold your advisor accountable is through a *fee-based* compensation structure, rather than by paying up-front commissions. With smaller ongoing fees, based on a percentage of assets under management, the advisor's interest is more aligned with your performance. Fee-based accounts generally have no cost or restrictions for leaving (i.e. they are *100% liquid* at all times).

Question #7

If I live (or move) out of town, how can we maintain a *personal feel* to our relationship, without meeting in person?

Preferred Answer:

"Our out-of-town clients participate in regular conference calls, portfolio & planning reviews, email exchanges, use of interactive technology, and periodic face-to-face visits."

Why this is Important:

Modern advisory practices should be adept at delivering excellent advice and service, regardless of being physically present for in-office, in-person meetings. While meeting face-to-face remains clients' *preferred* method of receiving financial and other planning advice, younger generations are shifting their venue expectations.

Look for a firm that has embraced technology-driven remote advice platforms. That firm is likely to stay current on most other economic and financial-related topics as well.

So if you happen to move out of town, after finding the right advisor, don't worry! Most reputable firms have the flexibility and technology to serve you no matter where you choose to live.

Special Note:

On a related note, you may have heard the term "robo-advice". Robo-Advisors are *automated* platforms that supplement - and occasionally *replace* - traditional financial advisory services. They are intended to cost less then traditional advice, and don't require face-to-face meetings.

These *robo-advisory* services are designed to provide basic asset allocation strategies using your financial data inputs. If you can log onto a computer, you can get some base-level advice. Many traditional advisors have recently embraced this technology to *supplement* their careful and thoughtful analysis. While these tools can be helpful, and certainly inexpensive, they should never take the place of a qualified professional advisor.

Financial planning is complex. While there is indeed a place in the market for user-friendly "app-like" investment tools, there is nothing more effective and valuable than the right financial coach.

Question #8

What *values* (moral codes, beliefs, ethics, etc.) are important to you and your firm?

Preferred Answer:

The values that you also hold dear.

There's not necessarily a *right* answer here, but you'll want to listen carefully to the advisor's response. It may provide you with a glimpse into the *character* of the people you're about to trust with your money. Hopefully, their values will align with yours, and it's best if they've thought enough about what's important to them to craft a written *Values Statement.*

Check your spirit (your gut-feeling) to get a sense of authenticity and genuineness... verses slyness and pandering. Discern whether you believe the firm actually *follows* these values, or has simply gone through the motions to *appear* more trustworthy.

Why this is Important:

Unfortunately, it's not uncommon for firms – especially financial services firms – to publicly say they adhere to the noblest of values, and then flatly *ignore* them in deeds and actions with your money. Values and morals are part of our very essence, the deep-rooted *core* of who we are as people. Finding an advisor who has *internalized* a set of positive values (knows them by heart and shares them passionately) is a good place to start your *financial courtship.*

Question #9

What happens if you retire, die, become disabled, or otherwise leave the firm? What is your succession plan?

Preferred Answer:

"Let me share with you our formal written plan for business continuity, and then introduce you to the people who would take over in my absence."

The advisor's answer should be clear and detailed, naming specific persons to takc over in the event he or she departs. They should be able to provide details about who will take over your account, and how that person will be made aware of your goals, objectives, resources, and needs.

Why this is Important:

If something were to happen to your advisor, you wouldn't want to start from scratch rebuilding your Financial Plan. Some circumstances causing an advisor to leave a firm are pre-planned, such as retirement. Other events are neither planned nor desirable, such as death or disability.

Shockingly, *many* financial advisors either have not seriously considered succession planning, or have neglected to put together a formal plan. Either way, make sure *your* advisor candidate has taken the time to personally develop possible successors – ones with expert knowledge and skills, and who share the firm's core values. If an advisor hasn't planned for his firm's own future, don't let them plan for yours.

Nine Questions To Ask

1- Who will be my primary point of contact for financial advice?

2- How do you measure performance?

3- How do you handle service requests?

4- Where will my money be held for safekeeping?

5- What's your perspective on *risk*, and what efforts will you take to understand mine?

6- Are there any costs or surrender penalties for leaving your firm or closing my account?

7- If I live out of town, how can we maintain a *personal feel* to our relationship, without meeting face-to-face?

8- What *values* (as in moral codes, beliefs, ethics, etc.) are important to you and your firm?

9- What happens if you retire, die, become disabled, or otherwise leave the firm? What's your succession plan?

About The Author

For over 20 years, Mike Gross has helped families and businesses secure financial independence. He works as a Certified Financial Planner, Retirement Plan Consultant, Investment Advisor, Teacher, and Writer out of Cornerstone's home office in Louisville, Kentucky.

Mike received his undergraduate degree from the University of Kentucky, majoring in Family Resource Management and Business, with an emphasis in Personal Finances. He earned a Master's Degree in Financial Planning from The American College's Irwin Graduate School. Mike is a Certified Financial Planner™ (CFP®), and a Certified Employee Benefit Specialist (CEBS®), with curriculum developed through The ISCEBS and The Wharton School at University of Pennsylvania. Mike is a Chartered Financial Consultant (ChFC®), a Certified Financial Manager (CFM), a Chartered Advisor for Seniors (CASL®), and a Qualified Retirement Plan Financial Consultant (QPFC). Mike is a credentialed member of the American Society of Pension Professionals and Actuaries (ASPPA) and a Member of the National Association of Plan Advisors (NAPA). Mike is also on the Board of the International Society of Certified Employee Benefits Specialists (ISCEBS) - Louisville Chapter, and is a member of the Louisville Employee Benefits Counsel (LEBC).

Mike has taught Financial and Retirement Planning classes to several of the region's largest employee groups. His specialties include: Qualified and Non-Qualified Retirement Plans, Personal Wealth Management, Tax Planning, Risk Management & Insurance, Executive Compensation, Trusts and Estates, Retirement Income Planning, Employee Group Benefits, Philanthropy & Planned Giving, and Investment Portfolio Analysis.

Mike lives in Louisville KY with his wife Sandy, where they enjoy spending time with kids, grandkids, and family. Mike loves the outdoors, enjoys hiking, biking, kayaking, and racing triathlons (including the 140.6-mile Ironman!). He is on the Board of YoungLife-Louisville, and is committed to several community, church, and faith-based organizations.

Made in the USA
Monee, IL
04 November 2026

67378659R00046